ANGELS

Chronicle Books · San Francisco

$\mathcal{T}$he archangel Raphael took the little wooden instrument out of Damiano's hands. He edged away along the bench, and his wings swept back in a businesslike manner. His face, as he retuned the strings, was chiselled perfectly, almost harsh in its perfection, unapproachable, forbidding . . . Slowly Raphael began to play the melody 'Ce fut en mai', which is a very simple tune, one he had helped Damiano to learn three years previously. He played it a number of times through, without trills, without ornamentation, without counterpoint of any kind. He did, however, play it differently . . .

Soon Damiano was utterly lost, as the angel struck the strings all together in what should have been a dissonant crash but was not. Raphael brushed the strings lightly, as though with his wings, and his left hand fluttered over the smooth black wood of the lute's neck. The sound was no longer music at all – unless water was music or the scraping of wind over the grass.

R. A. MacAvoy, *Damiano*

MELOZZO DA FORLI: ANGEL MUSICIAN

*A*nd is there care in Heaven? And is there love
   In heavenly spirits to these creatures base,
That may compassion of their evils move?
   There is: – else much more wretched were the case
   Of men than beasts: but O! th'exceeding grace
Of highest God, that loves his creatures so,
   And all his works with mercy doth embrace,
That blessed angels he sends to and fro,
To serve to wicked man, to serve his foe!

How oft do they their silver bowers leave
   To come to succour us that succour want!
How oft do they with golden pinions cleave
   The flitting skies, like flying pursuivant,
   Against foul fiends to aid us militant!
They for us fight, they watch and duly ward,
   And their bright squadrons round about us plant;
And all for love, and nothing for reward:
O! why should heavenly God to men have such regard?

Edmund Spenser, *The Ministry of Angels*

SANDRO BOTTICELLI: THE MYSTIC NATIVITY (DETAIL)

$\mathcal{I}$n the sixth month the angel Gabriel was sent from God to a city of Galilee named Nazareth, to a virgin betrothed to a man whose name was Joseph, of the house of David; and the virgin's name was Mary. And he came to her and said, 'Hail, O favoured one, the Lord is with you!' But she was greatly troubled at the saying, and considered in her mind what sort of greeting this might be. And the angel said to her, 'Do not be afraid, Mary, for you have found favour with God. And behold, you will conceive in your womb and bear a son, and you shall call his name Jesus. He will be great, and will be called the Son of the Most High, and the Lord God will give to him the throne of his father David, and he will reign over the house of Jacob for ever; and of his kingdom there will be no end.'

The Gospel According to Saint Luke

*T*wo angels, one of Life and one of Death,
   Passed o'er our village as the morning broke;
The dawn was on their faces, and beneath,
   The sombre houses hearsed with plumes of smoke.

Their attitude and aspect were the same,
   Alike their features and their robes of white;
But one was crowned with amaranth, as with flame,
   And one with asphodels, like flakes of light.

I saw them pause on their celestial way;
   Then said I, with deep fear and doubt oppressed,
'Beat not so loud, my heart, lest thou betray
   The place where thy beloved are at rest!'

Henry Wadsworth Longfellow, *The Two Angels*

*T*o reconcile the most romantic poignant Ideal of the heart with the severest practicality of thought and decision in its expression is one of the everlasting problems of Art – and we may say of Life. Everyone remembers the touching sentiment with which as a child he contemplated some nursery picture of an Angel, with outspread wings and a child in its arms, floating over a great city; or perhaps an engraving of Gustave Doré's 'Coliseum', with the lions prowling around the corpses below, and angelic beings floating above; or at the Public Gallery some celestial vision of Fra Angelico's. And everyone remembers the shock that came to the enquiring mind, as time went on – the child-like direct materialistic question, time and again set aside, and time and again recurring, with regard to these beautiful winged creatures – *how they put their clothes on?*

Edward Carpenter, *Angel's Wings*

EDWARD R. HUGHES: NIGHT AND HER TRAIN OF STARS

*L*et them praise Thy Name, let them praise Thee, the supercelestial people, Thine angels, who have no need to gaze up at this firmament, or by reading to know of Thy Word. For they always behold Thy face, and there read without any syllables in time, what willeth Thy eternal will; they read, they choose, they love. They are ever reading; and that never passes away which they read; for by choosing, and by loving, they read the very unchangeableness of Thy counsel. Their book is never closed, nor their scroll folded up; seeing Thou Thyself art this to them, and art eternally; because Thou hast ordained them above this firmament, which Thou hast firmly settled over the infirmity of the lower people, where they might gaze up and learn Thy mercy, announcing in time Thee Who madest times. For Thy mercy, O Lord, is in the heavens, and Thy truth reacheth unto the clouds. The clouds pass away, but the heaven abideth.

The Confessions of Saint Augustine

*A*bou Ben Adhem (may his tribe increase!)
    Awoke one night from a deep dream of peace,
And saw, within the moonlight in his room,
Making it rich, and like a lily in bloom,
An angel, writing in a book of gold: –
Exceeding peace had made Ben Adhem bold,
And to the presence in the room he said,
'What writest thou?' – The vision raised its head,
And, with a look made of all sweet accord,
Answered, 'The names of those who love the Lord.'
'And is mine one?' said Abou. 'Nay, not so,'
Replied the angel. Abou spoke more low,
But cheerly still; and said, 'I pray thee, then,
Write me as one that loves his fellow-men.'

The angel wrote, and vanished. The next night
It came again with a great wakening light,
And showed the names whom love of God had blessed,
And lo! Ben Adhem's name led all the rest.

Leigh Hunt, *Abou Ben Adhem and the Angel*

PIETRO CAVALLINI: THE LAST JUDGEMENT: SERAPHIM (DETAIL)

*O*n the first anniversary of the day Sir Galahad became king, the knights as usual went early to their prayers, but this time they found the Holy Grail out of the chest and a man kneeling before it in the appearance of a bishop, surrounded by a great fellowship of angels. The knights knelt, and the bishop began to celebrate the Eucharist. When he had consecrated, he turned to the knights and called Sir Galahad to him, saying: 'Come forth, servant of Jesus Christ, and you will see that which you have much desired to see.'

Then Sir Galahad began to tremble as in the mortal flesh he began to approach spiritual things. 'Lord, I thank Thee,' he said, 'for now I see that which has been my desire many a day.'

Therewith the bishop gave him the Sacrament.

Then Sir Galahad went to Sir Percivale and kissed him and commended him to God. Next he went to Sir Bors and kissed him and commended him to God and said: 'My fair lord, salute me unto my lord Sir Lancelot my father, and bid him remember me in this unstable world.'

A. M. Hadfield, *King Arthur and the Round Table*

$\mathscr{I}$ sat with Love upon a woodside well,
   Leaning across the water, I and he;
   Nor ever did he speak or look at me,
But touched his lute wherein was audible
The certain secret thing he had to tell:
   Only our mirrored eyes met silently
   In the low wave; and that sound came to be
The passionate voice I knew; and my tears fell.

And at their fall, his eyes beneath grew hers;
And with his foot and with his wing-feathers
   He swept the spring that watered my heart's drouth
Then the dark ripples spread to the waving hair,
And as I stooped, her own lips rising there
   Bubbled with brimming kisses at my mouth.

Dante Gabriel Rossetti, Willow-wood

GIOVANNI BATTISTA FIORENTINO: ANGEL MUSICIAN

*H*ark! the herald-angels sing
Glory to the new-born King.
Peace on earth, and mercy mild,
God and sinners reconciled.
Joyful all ye nations, rise,
Join the triumph of the skies;
With the Angelic host proclaim,
'Christ is born in Bethlehem.'
Hark! the herald-angels sing
Glory to the new-born King.

Christ, by highest Heav'n adored,
Christ, the Everlasting Lord,
Late in time behold Him come,
Offspring of a Virgin's womb.
Veil'd in flesh the Godhead see!
Hail, the Incarnate Deity!
Pleased as Man with man to dwell,
Jesus, our Emmanuel.

Charles Wesley, *Hark, the Herald Angels Sing*

ANON: THE WILTON DIPTYCH (DETAIL)

*B*urne-Jones does not shrink from the time-honoured, conventional angel, a human figure with physiologically impossible wings. Drapery and wings, indeed, are intermingled in a way that forbids us so much as to think of asking how such things can be. It is only by symbol that we can picture even our own powers. Do we not speak of swift-winged thought? And how else than by symbol shall we imagine, so that we may feel as if we were in the presence of, beings with higher powers than our own? Only those for whose thought man is the highest living being, and has no greater heights of being to reach, will be unhelped or offended by such symbols as Burne-Jones has used.

J. E. Phythian, *Burne-Jones*

*L*ittle Jesus, wast Thou shy
Once, and just so small as I?
And what did it feel like to be
Out of Heaven, and just like me?
Didst Thou sometimes think of *there*,
And ask where all the angels were?
I should think that I would cry
For my house all made of sky;
I would look about the air,
And wonder where my angels were;
And at waking 'twould distress me –
Not an angel there to dress me!

Hadst Thou ever any toys,
Like us little girls and boys?
And didst Thou play in Heaven with all
The angels, that were not too tall,
With stars for marbles? Did the things
Play 'Can you see me?' through their wings? . . .

Francis Thompson, *Ex Ore Infantium*

SIR JOSHUA REYNOLDS: ANGELS' HEADS (DETAIL)

I dreamt a dream! What can it mean?
And that I was a maiden Queen
Guarded by an Angel mild:
Witless woe was ne'er beguiled!

And I wept both night and day,
And he wiped my tears away;
And I wept both day and night,
And hid from him my heart's delight.

So he took his wings and fled;
Then the morn blushed rosy red.
I dried my tears, and armed my fears
With ten thousand shields and spears.

Soon my Angel came again;
I was armed, he came in vain;
For the time of youth was fled,
And grey hairs were on my head.

William Blake, *The Angel*

WILLIAM MORRIS: STAINED GLASS WINDOW OF A MINSTREL ANGEL, CATTISTOCK, DORSET (DETAIL)

*D*ear and great Angel, wouldst thou only leave
　　That child, when thou hast done with him, for me!
Let me sit all the day here, that when eve
　　Shall find performed thy special ministry
And time come for departure, thou, suspending
Thy flight, mayst see another child for tending,
　　Another still, to quiet and retrieve.

Then I shall feel thee step one step, no more,
　　From when thou standest now, to where I gaze,
– And suddenly my head is covered o'er
　　With those wings, white above the child who prays
Now on that tomb – and I shall feel thee guarding
Me, out of all the world; for me, discarding
　　Yon Heaven thy home, that waits and opes its door! . . .

Robert Browning, *The Guardian-Angel*

VINCENT VAN GOGH: HEAD OF AN ANGEL

I looked over Jordan, and what did I see,
Comin' for to carry me home,
A band of angels comin' after me,
Comin' for to carry me home.
  Swing low, sweet chariot,
  Comin' for to carry me home,
  Swing low, sweet chariot,
  Comin' for to carry me home.

If you get there before I do,
Comin' for to carry me home,
Tell all my friends I'm comin' too,
Comin' for to carry me home.
  Swing low, sweet chariot,
  Comin' for to carry me home,
  Swing low, sweet chariot,
  Comin' for to carry me home.

Anon., *Swing Low, Sweet Chariot*

HANS MEMLING: ANGEL MUSICIANS

First published in the United States in 1989
by Chronicle Books

Conceived, edited and designed by Russell Ash & Bernard Higton
Copyright © 1989 by Russell Ash & Bernard Higton

Printed in Hong Kong by Imago

ISBN 0-87701-716-6

Chronicle Books
275 Fifth Street
San Francisco, California
94103

Illustrations in order of appearance: Richard Bryant/Arcaid;
Vatican/Bridgeman Art Library; National Gallery; Museum
of San Marco, Florence/Scala; Wolfgang Lauter, Munich,
from: *Engel*, Die Bibliophilen Taschenbücher, Harenberg
Kommunikation, Dortmund, 1987; Birmingham City
Museum and Art Gallery; National Gallery; Santa Cecilia in
Travastere, Rome/Scala; Tate Gallery; Uffizi Gallery,
Florence/Scala; National Gallery; Tate Gallery; Tate Gallery;
Sonia Halliday & Laura Lushington; Private Collection/
Bridgeman Art Library; Antwerp Museum/Scala.
Text extracts from the following sources are reprinted with
the permission of their publishers: R.A. MacAvoy, *Damiano*,
Bantam, 1988; A.M. Hadfield, *King Arthur and the Round
Table*, J.M. Dent & Sons, 1953.